SCANDINAVIAN FIGURE CARVINGS

From the Viking Era to Döderhultarn, Trygg, and Modern Carvers

BY HARLEY REFSAL

A *Woodcarving Illustrated* Book
www.WoodcarvingIllustrated.com

FOX CHAPEL
PUBLISHING

© 2015 by Harley Refsal and Fox Chapel Publishing Company, Inc., East Petersburg, PA.

ISBN 978-1-56523-875-6

Library of Congress Cataloging-in-Publication Data

Refsal, Harley.
  [Art & technique of Scandinavian-style woodcarving]
  Scandinavian figure carvings / Harley Refsal.
     pages cm
  Scandinavian Figure Carvings is a revised and updated version of Art & Technique of Scandinavian Style Woodcarving.
  Includes index.
  ISBN 978-1-56523-875-6
  1. Wood-carving--Scandinavia. 2. Wood-carved figurines--Scandinavia. I. Title.
  TT199.7.R4396 2015
  736'.40948--dc23
                    2015014552

To learn more about the other great books from Fox Chapel Publishing,
or to find a retailer near you, call toll-free
800-457-9112 or visit us at *www.FoxChapelPublishing.com*.

Note to Authors: We are always looking for talented authors to write new books. Please send a brief letter
describing your idea to Acquisition Editor, 1970 Broad Street, East Petersburg, PA 17520.

Printed in Singapore
First printing

ICELAND

NORWAY

Early carvings displayed in Sandvig
Collection at Maihaugen Museum

Lillehammer

Site of early carvings

*Rauland in
Telemark*

Oslo

DENMARK

Home of
Dalecarlian horse

Mora

SWEDEN

Stockholm

Oskarshamn

Home of
Axel Petersson Döderhultarn

FINLAND

ESTONIA

RUSSIA

LATVIA

LITHUANIA

BELARUS

UNITED KINGDOM

NETHERLANDS

BELGIUM

GERMANY

POLAND

UKRAINE

LIECHTENSTEIN

FRANCE

Contents

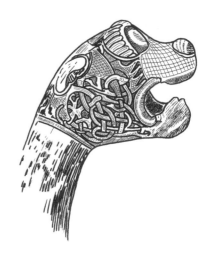

Axel Petersson Döderhultarn

Döderhultarn's Influence on Other Carvers

Carl Johan Trygg

Oscar Sjogren

Herman Rosell

Emil Janel
Thelma "Telle" Rudser

Sven and Urban Gunnarsson

Martin Engseth

Bjarne Walle

Henning Engelsen

Anton Pearson

Other Scandinavian Carvers

Richard Rolander

Andy Anderson

Harold Enlow

Harley Refsal

CHAPTER 3
Carving a Traditional Dalecarlian Horse 66

About the Author

Harley Refsal is an internationally recognized figure carver who specializes in Scandinavian-style flat-plane carving. In 1996, he received the St. Olav Medal from the King of Norway in recognition of his contributions to Norwegian folk art. In 2012, Harley was named the Woodcarver of the Year by *Woodcarving Illustrated* magazine for both reviving the art of flat-plane carving and teaching it across the United States and around the world.

Now the Professor Emeritus of Scandinavian Folk Art at Luther College in Decorah, Iowa, Harley was born and raised on the farm near Hoffman, Minnesota, that was homesteaded by his Norwegian-immigrant grandparents. He began working in wood as a young boy. His father, who was a carpenter and farmer, and a woodworker uncle who lived nearby kept Harley well supplied with wood, tools, and encouragement.

Primarily self-taught, Harley began winning awards in regional and national carving exhibitions in the late 1970s. He also began researching the history of Scandinavian flat-plane carving, with which he had become especially enamored. But soon he discovered that most of the artists who had worked in this style during the height of its popularity in the early decades of the 20th century in both Scandinavia and America had died, and the tradition of flat-plane carving had faded to near-extinction.

Since the 1980s, Harley, who speaks fluent Norwegian, has shared his knowledge of, and skills in, Scandinavian flat-plane carving with thousands of carvers in classes and presentations in North America and Scandinavia. In addition to writing several books on the subject, he has authored many book chapters and magazine articles, and has been featured on numerous radio and television programs, including the PBS Peabody Award-winning series *Craft in America*. His name is so integrally linked with the revival of this carving style that it is often referred to as the "Refsal style."

Preface

In this book, the discussion of Scandinavian-style figure carving, and "flat-plane" carving in particular, will deal with a style of carving that developed and became popular in Norway and Sweden. Although Denmark, Finland, and Iceland also comprise part of Scandinavia, I am limiting the discussion to Norway and Sweden because their conditions and traditions are fairly similar—especially, as we shall see, when it comes to figure carving. Therefore, in the context of this book, the term "Scandinavian" will refer only to Norway and Sweden. The style of figure carving I will be discussing was common in both countries, but it was far less common in Denmark and Finland and nearly nonexistent in Iceland.

The term "flat-plane carving" stems from a particular style of figure carving—one in which large, flat planes, created by using primarily a knife and perhaps just a gouge or two, were left intact. Smooth, rounded sculpting and sanding were typically not employed in the final finish.

I was introduced to Scandinavian figure carving during my first visit to Norway in 1965. Two years later, while studying at the University of Oslo, I was able to travel more widely throughout Norway as well as in Sweden. Because I had worked with wood and had also done some whittling as a boy, I became interested in the woodcarving traditions of both countries. I was especially intrigued by the small wooden figures I saw in shops and museums.

Upon returning to the United States in 1968, I began to carve figures of my own, using a pocketknife and a wood chisel that my father, a carpenter and farmer, had made from a worn-out file. Because I was unable to locate any carvers creating the style of figures I had seen in Scandinavia, I simply gleaned what information and inspiration I could from photos, articles, and sketches I had made.

One of the articles I eventually ran across featured photos of some carvings by Axel Petersson Döderhultarn, whose rough-hewn figures have made a lasting impression on me. Using only a few well-placed cuts and leaving large flat planes, he was able to convey fascinating stories in wood.

I had been attempting to tell stories through my figures too, and Döderhultarn's style of carving provided just the means of expression I had been seeking. I began using this style of carving to create objects and figures with which I was familiar, and I began trying to say more by saying less.

Since that first visit in 1965, I have traveled in Norway and Sweden on many occasions. By the early 1980s, however, I noticed that fewer figures carved in this flat-plane style were available in shops.

Meanwhile, I had been carving a great deal in the United States and teaching courses and workshops on Scandinavian-style figure carving since the early 1980s. So when my family and I moved to Norway in 1988, where I was enrolled in a graduate program of folk art studies, I was eager to explore the figure carving tradition further. I also hoped to locate carvers who were still creating figures in this style. But I eventually learned that the tradition had become almost extinct, and I couldn't locate a single course being taught on the subject, either in Norway or Sweden.

Therefore, when I was asked if I would teach a week-long course at the school I was attending, I readily accepted. Since 1988, I have taught numerous courses and workshops in Norway on flat-plane carving and am pleased to see that there is now a growing number of Scandinavian, as well as American and Canadian, carvers who are carving once again in that style.

During the year my family and I lived in Norway, I traveled throughout Norway and Sweden, gathering additional information about the tradition and its practitioners. I am happy to be able to share with you in this book what I have learned.

After having taught courses throughout the United States as well as in Scandinavia, I can't decide which I enjoy more—carving figures myself or trying to help others develop their skills so that they can tell their own stories in wood. But I can say with certainty that my admiration for the small wooden figures that whispered into my ear a half-century ago only keeps on growing.

—Harley Refsal

Auction, by Axel Petersson Döderhultarn.

Buying and Collecting Scandinavian Carvings

Although you can occasionally buy vintage or antique Scandinavian-style carvings at antique shops and local galleries, or on eBay, serious collectors turn to expert dealers. Little known to many North American collectors, Bukowskis is the leading art business in the Nordic countries and the largest auction house in Scandinavia. The company was very generous in sharing photography for the book. In addition, Lisa Gartz, Bokowskis' specialist in Old Master paintings and sculptures, shared some advice on collecting Scandinavian carvings.

Expert Advice

By Lisa Gartz, Specialist Old Master Paintings and Sculptures

Q: What is the collectibility and value of the auction pieces offered by Bukowskis in Scandinavia?

A: Axel Petersson Döderhultarn is extremely popular in Sweden; everyone is familiar with the artist. His work is featured at every auction. In the 1980s and 1990s, the value of the carvings was much higher—values have declined in recent years.

Q: What was the peak sales record for a carving by Axel Petersson Döderhultarn?

A: The most lucrative piece, The Court, was sold in 2004 for EUR 61,000 (approximately $76,000 at the time). Another piece, The Wedding, was sold in 1989 for EUR 22,000 (approximately $19,800). Most group pieces will sell for EUR 5,000–6,000 ($5,620–$6,745) now, comparatively. Single figures will sell for approximately EUR 1,000 ($1,125) each.

Q: What is the popularity of animal figures vs. human figures?

A: Animals tend to be more popular. Horse and cows are most sought after.

Q: Any problems with counterfeiting?

A: Yes, they are imitated, but the auctioneers and experts can detect a fraud easily.

Q: Are there other folk-art carvers of similar popularity?

A: Perhaps in the 1970s, but in today's market, no one can compare.

Grazing Cow, by Axel Petersson Döderhultarn

Photo by Bukowskis auctions.

Q: How can the public go about buying through Bukowskis?

A: Art by Döderhultarn is available for bid every other week through internet auctions. A sale is held twice a year that features the more costly pieces. The live auctions are available in more than 182 countries.

About Bukowskis

One of the oldest salesrooms for fine art in Scandinavia, Bukowskis was founded in 1870 by a Polish nobleman, Hendry Bukowski, and has conducted auctions in Sweden for the past 140 years. The company has sold many great collections, from that of King Charles XV in 1873 to the estate of the film director Ingmar Bergman in 2009. During the 1920s, Bukowskis enjoyed the sole right to sell the etchings by one of the best-known Swedish classical artists, Anders Zorn, which established the company in the fine-art category.

Bukowskis' headquarters are in Stockholm. However, the firm has branches and representatives across Europe, the United States, and Asia. They also offer online auctions and private sales. Learn more about Bukowskis and see their collections of fine art, including carvings, at www.bukowskis.com and www.bukowskismarket.com.

Viewing the Carvings

If you are interested in viewing and enjoying significant collections of Scandinavian-style figures firsthand, consider visiting these museums in the United States, Sweden, and Norway.

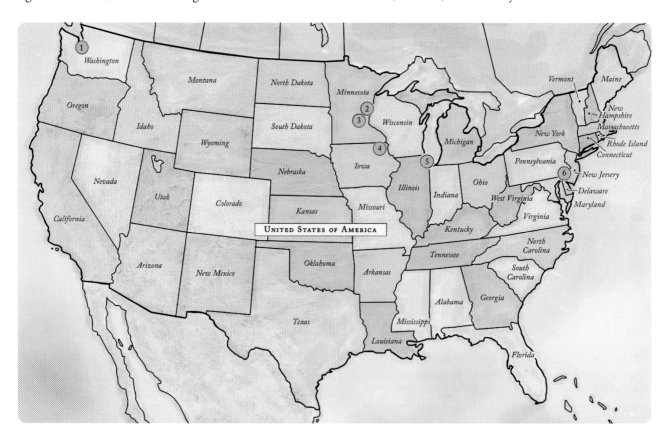

1. Nordic Heritage Museum
3014 N.W. 67th St.
Seattle, WA 98117
www.nordicmuseum.org
Countless 19th century emigrants from Norway and Sweden were initially drawn to the American Midwest, due to the availability of inexpensive (or free—thanks to the Homestead Act of 1862) farm land. Later, however, many continued moving farther west. Through its permanent collection of more than 65,000 items, the Nordic Heritage Museum presents not only the general immigration story, but also focuses specifically on immigrant life in the Pacific Northwest.

2. Gammelgården
20880 Olinda Trail N.
Scandia, MN 55073
www.gammelgardenmuseum.org
A small, wonderfully preserved and restored farmstead and open-air museum, less than an hour's drive north of Minneapolis–St. Paul, Gammelgården ("Old Farm") offers a look into the life and material culture of 19th century Swedish immigrants to the rural Midwest.

3. American Swedish Institute
2600 Park Ave S.
Minneapolis, MN 55407
www.asimn.org
ASI, a museum and cultural center in the heart of Minneapolis, has a highly impressive and comprehensive

collection of Scandinavian-style carved figures. Creations by notables such as Döderhultarn, the Tryggs, Herman Rosell, and Emil Janel (dozens of pieces) are all there, and well represented. A recent addition to the historic Turnblad Mansion provides space for exhibits of contemporary Nordic art and culture, as well as classroom space.

4. Vesterheim Norwegian-American Museum
520 W. Water St.
Decorah, IA 52101
www.vesterheim.org
Vesterheim (Norwegian for "Western Home" or "Home in the West") derives its name from the term countless 19th century Norwegians gave to the American Midwest; a place across the sea where the majority had family members or friends. Today's Vesterheim consists of 12 buildings in Decorah, approximately a three-hour drive from Minneapolis–St. Paul. A wide variety of handwork courses are offered throughout the year.

5. Swedish American Museum
5211 N. Clark St.
Chicago, IL 60640
www.SwedishAmericanMuseum.org
The Museum's permanent exhibit, The Dream of America: Swedish Immigration to Chicago, dramatizes the story of immigrants to an urban, rather than a farming, area. Their stories are told in words as well as in the items (including, not surprisingly, numerous wooden items) they brought along. Special exhibits focus on a variety of themes.

6. American Swedish Historical Museum
1900 Pattison Ave.
Philadelphia, PA 19145
www.americanswedish.org
A community named New Sweden began to take root in the New World as early as 1638, centuries before large-scale 19th century Swedish emigration began. This museum's permanent collection shares that fascinating story, and temporary exhibits and activities focus on a wide variety of themes relating to Swedish and Swedish-American life and culture.

7. Norsk Folkemuseum / Norwegian Folk Museum
Museumsveien 20
0287 Oslo, Norway
www.norskfolkemuseum.no
Norway's largest cultural history museum features a permanent collection of 160 historic (mainly log) buildings, all furnished, largely with wooden items, that tell the story of daily life in a primarily rural Norway from the 1500s until modern times. Gol Stave Church was built in about 1200. Larger buildings house permanent collections focusing on folk art, old toys, and Sami handwork, as well as rotating special exhibitions.

8. Maihaugen
Maihaugvegen 1
2609 Lillehammer, Norway
www.maihaugen.no
Founded in 1887 by a dentist, Anders Sandvig, the open-air museum features approximately 200 buildings. Most of them are log farm buildings that were purchased, moved to the site, and re-erected, along with their original furnishings. A wide variety of carved wooden items are featured.

9. Museet Svenska Trägubbar / Swedish Figure Carving Museum
Falköpingsvägen 7
565 32 Mullsjö, Sweden
www.tragubbarna.se
This private museum was founded by, and houses the collection of, an enthusiastic figure carving collector and carver. His collection—which features the work of dozens of carvers, including his own—now includes over 1,800 carved figures, mainly caricatures. The museum, begun in 2008, is open seasonally (days and hours listed on the website) and by appointment.

10. Dalarnas Museum / County Museum of Dalarna
Stigargatan 2-4
791 21 Falun, Sweden
www.dalarnasmuseum.se
An important role in the Nordic figure carving tradition features the famous Dala horse, a once-humble carved wooden toy that eventually grew up to become the informal national symbol of Sweden. "Dala" is short for Dalarna, the province in central Sweden where the tradition began. The Dalarna Museum houses the world's largest and most comprehensive permanent collection of Dala horses in the world.

11. Nordiska Museet
Djurgårdsvägen 6-16
SE 115 93 Stockholm, Sweden
www.nordiskamuseet.se

This museum of cultural history, with over 1.5 million items in its permanent collections, is the largest and most comprehensive of its kind in the country, documenting life in Sweden from the 1500s to the present. Folk and traditional arts, including wooden and wood-carved items, are prominently featured. Skansen (www.skansen.se), a nearby open-air museum, features restored buildings moved from all over Sweden, staffed by attendants and demonstrators in period dress.

FOLK FESTIVALS AND HERITAGE EVENTS

A quick search of the internet reveals a dizzying array of Scandinavian cultural festivals across the United States and Scandinavia, featuring food, dance, fine art, clothing, and, yes, carving. As much as I would have liked to list them here, I find that the dates, locations, sponsors, and contact information for even the well-established events change from year to year. When you find them, though, they are good fun, so I encourage you to search for festivals near you, and to attend. (Note: While some wonderful festivals use the word "Nordic" in their titles or descriptions, be warned that a few events unrelated to Scandinavian heritage have adopted the term, as well. Search with caution and research the event before traveling to attend.)

CHAPTER 1

The History of Scandinavian Figure Carving

Before focusing our attention on Scandinavian figure carving, it is important to consider the general context in which this particular folk art emerged. As we shall see, wood chips were flying in Scandinavia long before figure carving became popular there.

Viking Era and Medieval Carving

Our earliest examples of woodcarving in Scandinavia date back to the Viking era (ca. 800–1050 A.D.). Already back then, woodcarving had reached a high level of achievement, as indicated by the items found buried with the Oseberg Ship, now housed at the Viking Ship Museum in Oslo. The Oseberg Ship was named after the Norwegian farm that was on the land from which the ship was excavated. Buried with the ship were vehicles and furniture and all kinds of household and personal items. Thus, the excavation, conducted in 1904, yielded a unique look into the past, providing us with a time capsule thought to date from the first half of the ninth century.

The items decorated with carving include the ship itself, a horse-drawn carriage, and three sledges. In terms of the motifs, there are relief-carved animal ornamentations, geometric designs, and some three-dimensional figure carving. The high quality of the carving from the Oseberg excavation suggests that woodcarving must have been a leading form of art in the Viking era.

Another excavated Viking ship, the Gokstad Ship, can also be seen at the Viking Ship Museum. Dating from around 900 A.D., this ship also contained some carved items, including parts of a bed frame that features the relief-carved head of an animal, possibly a horse. In addition, the head of an animal or beast of some kind, carved three-dimensionally, appears on one of the ship's oarlocks. Both the bed frame and the oarlock were rendered in a mode of carving that has become known as the Borre style. Named after a burial mound on a Norwegian farm called Borre, this style was widespread both in Norway and Sweden.

Wooden stave churches (named for the large staves, or pillars, in their support structure), built in Norway from ca. 1000 to 1300 A.D., also featured examples of woodcarving. Of the estimated one to two thousand stave churches once found throughout the country, only about thirty have survived. But decorative carving from these churches provides us with yet another excellent source of Norway's rich carving heritage. Animal and plant motifs, especially around doorways and on pillars, were common. The motifs often blended native and foreign elements, drawing some of their impulses from classical traditions common throughout other parts of Europe.

The carving found on stave churches, as well as from earlier Viking-era ship finds, was undoubtedly done by trained artists, some of whom may have worked under royal patronage. As the stave-church era

Opposite:
Horse and Rider, 1830.

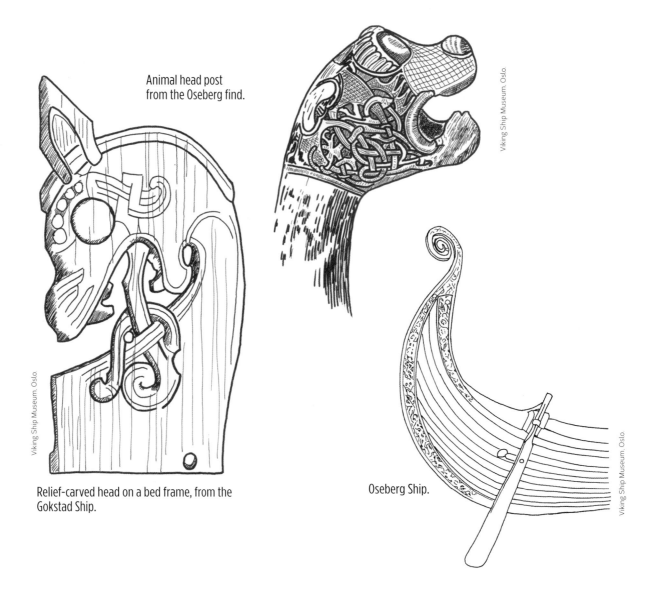

Animal head post from the Oseberg find.

Relief-carved head on a bed frame, from the Gokstad Ship.

Oseberg Ship.

progressed, local carvers also may have been trained on site to do some of the carving, but most of the work from this period was done by specialists, not by "common folk" who simply picked up a tool and began to carve.

The tools available to Viking-era carvers certainly must have included gouges and curved knives in addition to simple straight-carving, or all-purpose, knives. It is impossible for the intricate relief work found in the Oseberg excavation as well as on stave church portals and doors to have been done using only a knife. A woodcarving tool from the Middle Ages found in an excavation near Tønsberg, Norway, suggests that a wide variety of tools had been developed and were available to carvers at that time. Therefore, we must conclude that

similar tools were available several hundreds of years earlier as well.

There is very little evidence of "art for art's sake" from the Viking era. Some small figures, carved primarily in bone, ivory, or stone, which were undoubtedly of cultic or religious significance, have been discovered. Also, a few gaming pieces, such as the carved-ivory chess pieces known as the Lewis Chess Set (now in the British Museum in London), have been found (page 19). But, in the main, the carving during the Viking era was decorative or applied art on functional objects.

It is, of course, possible that carved wooden objects, including figures, were far more common than the evidence suggests. But due to the nature of the material, wood, most would have rotted away long ago. However, one excavation site at Kvivik on the Faroe Islands, settled by Scandinavians during the Viking era, has yielded two tantalizing wooden horses and two small wooden boats, probably created for use as children's toys. One can only speculate about the identity of the carver, or carvers, of these objects. The simplified, almost crude, pieces could certainly have been carved with only a knife, so perhaps just a "common person," handy with a knife, created them.

On the whole, however, the rich carving tradition practiced in Scandinavia approximately seven hundred to a thousand years ago was carried on by trained artists. Yet, as we shall see, their work lived on to inspire countless self-taught craftsmen, who studied the Viking era and medieval motifs and began replicating them on their farms and in their homes.

Eidsborg Stave Church, Telemark, Norway, ca. 1300.

From Stave Church to Storehouse: The Emergence of Folk Art

Scandinavia, along with much of the rest of the world, was ravaged by the Black Death, or bubonic plague, in the mid-fourteenth century. It is estimated that more than half of the population died, after which large parts of Scandinavia, especially Norway, were laid waste for several generations. Artistic development was severely curtailed, as the people were devastated and had to spend virtually all of their time simply eking out a living. It wasn't until a couple of centuries had passed that the people were back on their feet to the extent that they could think about devoting time to aesthetically enhancing their surroundings.

The populations of Norway and Sweden have historically been overwhelmingly agrarian. Only a very small percentage of the people lived in towns, a situation that remained true well into the nineteenth century, when the Industrial Revolution began to create jobs in factories. Prior to that, most people lived on self-sufficient farms, where all of their buildings, vehicles, tools, furniture, and utensils were made of wood, right there on the farms.

At least well into the eighteenth century, Scandinavian farmers were largely illiterate, had no formal art training, lacked travel opportunities, and had few, if any, pictures or books at their disposal. So, farmers who wanted to decorate a building or household object turned for inspiration to designs they saw firsthand in their own communities. In some parts of Sweden, inspiration could have been drawn from nearby manor houses or castles. In other parts of Sweden, as well as in Norway, inspiration often came from churches. After viewing a professionally carved candle holder, baptismal font, pulpit, or portal, countless farmers returned to their homes and modeled drinking vessels, candle holders, utensils, or other household objects on what they had seen. In Sweden, and especially in Norway, with its numerous ornately carved stave churches, farmers began to replicate pillars and doorways from churches on their storage buildings, virtually all of which were made of logs. Carved ornamentation also began to appear on their houses.

In addition to scroll-like plant motifs and geometric designs, majestic and haunting images of animals figured prominently in architectural carving. Lions were

St. Göran, Lögdö Chapel, Medelpad, Sweden, early 1500s.

Detail from doorframe, Gol Stave Church, ca. 1200.

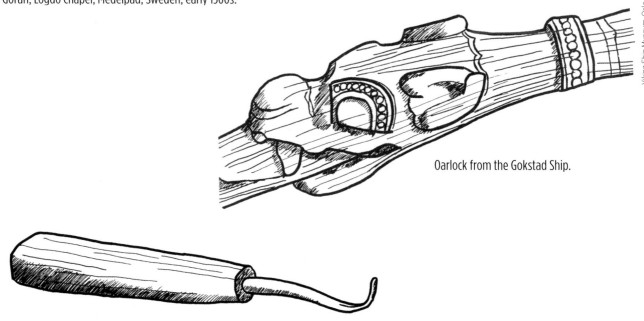

Oarlock from the Gokstad Ship.

Carving tool from the Middle Ages, found near Tønsberg, Norway.

Craftsman with knife and axe.

Viking-era carver.

especially common. Originally a symbol of kingship in the Orient, the lion motif made its way, with returning crusaders, to the European continent, where it became a common element in heraldry. Over time, the theme was picked up by other artists on the Continent, including carvers, and eventually lions found their way into Scandinavian design—first as deep-relief carvings mounted on doorposts of stave churches and later on storage buildings, furniture, and tools.

This phenomenon of untrained artists adopting the designs and motifs of earlier artists and then reinterpreting and creating them in their local setting is a good example of what we now call "folk art." Folk art was also referred to as "peasant art" early in the twentieth century, because it was typically made by rural folk of meager means who had to create and decorate their possessions themselves, rather than purchase them. In the Scandinavian context, folk art was basically the art used on utilitarian objects, including everything

from buildings and vehicles to utensils and toys, that were created by the people in the general population, who drew their inspiration from the designs they saw around them.

Two main types of art existed simultaneously during this "Golden Age of Scandinavian Folk Art" (ca. 1700–1850). Urban, or "international," art thrived among the rather small upper class, while more of a peasant art flourished in the heavily populated rural areas.

It is of interest to note that from the sixteenth through the eighteenth century, farmers and other rural craftsmen who were creating folk art had relatively few tools at their disposal. Specialized tools for carving, fine woodworking, and joinery were jealously hoarded by the small groups of urban craftsmen, most of whom were in the guild system. In Norway, a royal decree from the Danish king (Norway was under Denmark's rule from 1380 to 1814) actually made it illegal for farmers throughout the country to use

Carved wooden baptismal font from Telemark, Norway, Middle Ages.

Kubbestol (chair made from a hollowed log), Hallingdal, Norway, before 1873.

refined tools. In an effort to thwart competition with the trained craftsmen of the government-controlled guild system, farmers were forbidden to use tools other than knives and axes—tools deemed sufficient for basic but rough construction of log buildings, simple furniture, and farm implements. Many farmers obviously ignored the decree, which was in effect for about a hundred years, from the late seventeenth to the late eighteenth century, and made or bartered for fine woodworking tools. Still, the ban was somewhat effective, and much of the work done by rural craftsmen during that era reflects the limited range of tools at their disposal.

However, if one has only a couple of tools available, one can develop amazing skill with just those tools, and some highly impressive work was created during that period with just a knife and an axe. The story is told in the Norwegian county of Telemark about a man who was seeking employment as a log builder. Having just wandered into a community, he was directed to a site where a log building was under construction. The man approached the foreman about a job, but the foreman was hesitant and asked the stranger if he could handle an axe. Without saying a word, the stranger walked over to a chopping block, spread apart the fingers of his left hand and laid it palm-down on the block. He then proceeded to chop into the block four times, striking the axe perfectly in the spaces between his outstretched fingers. When he was finished, the foreman said, "You can start right over there on the far corner!"

Wood: The Universal Material

Norway and Sweden are richly endowed with forests. Nearly half of Sweden and a quarter of Norway are covered with pine, spruce, and birch. Due to the cool climate afforded by the Scandinavian Peninsula's northerly latitude, trees grow slowly and are typically not harvested until they are seventy-five to one hundred and fifty years old. Annual growth rings are therefore close together, providing ideal material for woodwork of all kinds.

Almost everything was made out of wood in traditional, rural Scandinavian society. In addition to buildings and vehicles, objects that we today regard more as hardware items, such as hinges, pails, tools and fencing materials, and even shoes were made primarily from wood.

Instead of searching for a tree that would provide that "nice, straight board," farmers and craftsmen often chose a suitably curved or twisted piece instead. A branch from a gnarled mountain birch tree that had been deformed through years of buffeting by wind and snow might yield

Pieces from the Lewis Chess Set, made of walrus ivory, 1200s.

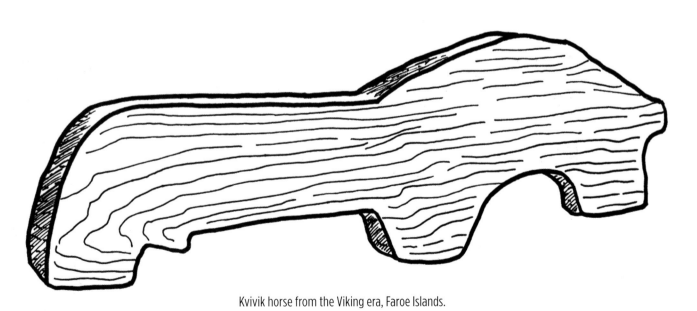

Kvivik horse from the Viking era, Faroe Islands.

Log storehouse, Telemark, Norway.

Lion detail on portal of Eidsborg Stave Church, Telemark, Norway, ca. 1300.

just the perfect shape from which a hinge, C-clamp, or plow beam could be made. A naturally bent limb with the grain following the shape is, of course, stronger than a piece of wood that one could create into that shape artificially. Thus, a plow beam made from a six- to seven-inch-thick, naturally bent birch branch fitted with an iron tip proved to be nearly as strong as one made entirely from metal.

Burls were also widely used. The grain in a burl does not run in only one direction but appears to swirl around almost randomly, so burls provided ideal material from which to carve bowls and scoops.

Contemporary rendition of traditional Norwegian knife and sheath, made by Norma Refsal, 1989.

Bowls were often turned on a lathe, but free-form shapes were also created, carved from a crotch or a burl. Ale bowls, sometimes carved in the shapes of hens or geese, were used for ceremonial drinking, especially in connection with weddings, funerals, and other ceremonies or festivities. Some bird-shaped ale bowls were carved with rounded bottoms, and they would be floated on the surface of the ale in a larger wooden container. They served as floating dippers, from which one could either drink directly or pour the ale into another container.

Due to their ceremonial use, ale bowls were frequently decorated with carving or painting. Other bowls, however, were often shaped according to the piece of wood from which they were carved, with the shape itself providing the design.

Horse hames or other harness fittings and parts were also made using naturally bent or curved pieces of wood—preferably birch, because of its strength—and were frequently decorated, as well. The harness saddle

Wooden plow with iron plowshare. Rauland, Telemark, Norway.

Bent birch tree in Rauland, Norway.

C-clamp, made from a naturally formed piece of birch. Rauland, Norway.

shown on page 23, originally from a farm in the Swedish province of Ångermanland and now on view at the Nordiska Museet, Stockholm, is a good example of the use of a naturally curved piece of wood. A component of the harness also exemplifies the use of the lion motif that was mentioned earlier.

Clogs, or wooden shoes, provide yet another example of articles commonly made from wood. Although we associate wooden shoes primarily with Holland, clogs have been worn since the Middle Ages in many parts of Europe, including Norway and Sweden. Even after the introduction of the more expensive leather boots and shoes, wooden clogs continued to be popular because they could be made locally and were so convenient. You simply stepped into them and walked off. Clogs were often lined with hay or straw, both for cushioning and for warmth. The pair pictured on page 24, believed to have been made in Scandinavia and brought to the United States by immigrants who settled near Hoffman, Minnesota, was even fitted for winter traction, complete with hand-forged metal spikes on the bottom.

Many of these articles, intended for everyday use, were decorated. Employing chip carving, relief work, incised carving, and/or woodburning, traditional craftsmen transformed hinges, drinking vessels, ladles, and harness parts into articles that were also aesthetically pleasing. "The eye also has its needs" is an expression that craftsmen regularly took to heart.

As we can see, even though it is difficult to document a figure-carving tradition, per se, within Scandinavian folk art that goes back more than a few hundred years, the stage had been set long before. Wood had been a universal material for centuries. It would only be a matter of time before craftsmen familiar with the material and skilled with knives would begin turning their attention to carving objects other than just utilitarian items.

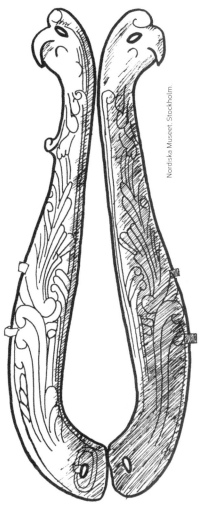

Ale ladle from Setesdal, Norway.

Horse hames from Småland, Sweden.

The Emergence of Carved Figures and the Dalecarlian Horse

The earliest carved human or animal figures in this folk art tradition were probably used as protective or good-luck charms. Some were mounted inside houses, whereas others stood guard in storage buildings.

Two figures from a farm called Heggtveit Vestre in Telemark, Norway, are noteworthy examples of such charms. One of the figures, a husgud (house god), approximately six inches tall and featuring the head of a human, was originally fastened high up on the interior wall of the house. Believed to date from the Middle Ages, it is one of the oldest and finest examples we have of a house god in Norway. It resembles the kind of figure,

perhaps a saint, commonly found on walls or pillars inside churches.

The second figure, a horse and rider, pictured on page 13, was prominently placed as a protective or good-luck charm on the second floor of the Heggtveit farm's storehouse. The 1830 date painted on the horse's stomach, together with the rider's dress, suggests that the figure represented a government official or military man, perhaps attached to the Telemark Company in nearby Dalen. In 1830, Swedish military uniforms were being worn in Norway, because Norway was united with Sweden from 1814 to 1905. The rider's outstretched hand has a small hole drilled through it, indicating that some

Nordiska Museet. Stockholm

Horse from Dalarna, 1840s.

Container from Sogn, Norway, decorated with a combination
of woodburning and chip carving.

Nordiska Museet. Stockholm

Harness saddle from Ångermanland, Sweden.

object, perhaps a flag on a flagpole, was originally part of the carving.

A candle holder in the form of a lion (see page 27) now in the Sandvig Collection at Maihaugen in Lillehammer, Norway, harks back to the lion motif that was mentioned earlier. The piece was originally from a farm near Ringebu in Gudbrandsdalen.

Another figure in the Maihaugen Collection, an elegant horse made by the famous eighteenth-century carver Kristen Erlandsen Listad (1726-1802), is technically a toy, but one of those toys that children undoubtedly had to handle very carefully. The Listad horse was featured in a commemorative stamp in 1987, the one hundredth anniversary of the Sandvig Collection.

Another horse (pictured on page 26) was carved in approximately 1825 by Anne Hellem of Gransherad, Telemark. This carving, also undoubtedly created for use as a toy, is fairly unique in that it was made by a woman. Carving, as well as woodwork in general, was typically done by men, whereas women devoted themselves more to textiles.

The carving of wooden animals and human figures by common folk in Sweden is traceable back more than two hundred years. It can be readily documented since about 1840, with the emergence of the now-world-famous Dalecarlian horse, an object that has become Sweden's unofficial national symbol. The province of Dalarna, and especially the community of Mora, had long been a center for the building of wooden clock cases, and the horses whittled from the scraps leftover from the clock cases gradually became an economic mainstay for countless families.

Even earlier than the 1840s, however, men working in lumber camps often lived far back in the woods and were separated from their families for weeks or months at a time. As a way of using their free time during the long winter evenings and in order to be able to bring toys home for their children, the men often whittled horses or other figures. Although roosters and pigs were not uncommon objects, horses were favored by carvers as well as by the children who received them. These figures, some of which can be seen in the Nordiska Museet in Stockholm and in various provincial museums, were painted in colorful floral motifs or sometimes left unpainted. The horse from Dalarna shown on page 23 was originally painted, but years of use by small hands have nearly obliterated the coloration and given it a warm, dark patina.

As previously mentioned, it was near Mora that large-scale production of the Dalarna figures began in about 1840. The carving of the figures, primarily horses, was done by local craftsmen in their homes. Working in pine or spruce, a good carver could produce a dozen horses per day, using a hatchet and a knife as his only tools. Flat-plane carving, with visible tool marks, was the result. The figures were usually left unsanded.

The painting was done by specialists who often drew their inspiration for designs from the horses featured in

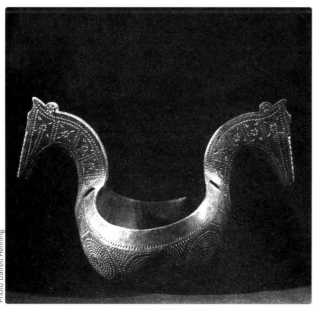

Norwegian ale bowl, possibly late eighteenth century. Vesterheim/Luther College Collection, Decorah, Iowa.

Wooden shoes, with metal spikes on the bottom.

Doorframe detail on storehouse, Telemark, ca. 1300.

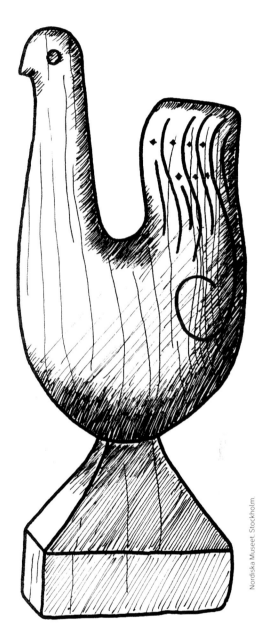

Rooster from Dalarna, 1840s.

the well-known wall paintings in the area. Many of these wall paintings seem to have received their inspiration from illustrations in the so-called "Gustav Adolf's Bible" of the 1580s. The styles of saddles and martingales, as well as the combination of colors chosen by the painters of the wooden horses, suggest that wall paintings significantly influenced many of the painters.

It is interesting to note that as long ago as the 1840s, the Dalecarlian horse had already become a popular item throughout Sweden. When Mora-area craftsmen traveled by horse and wagon to other parts of the country to sell their locally produced clocks, baskets, or spinning wheels, they typically had along a good supply of carved horses, which they used as payment for their room and board. The figures thus became a kind of currency. Frequently the horses, which were meant to be used as toys, were given to the children of the farmer or innkeeper with whom they stayed. In addition to paying for lodging, the horses were also commonly traded for such items as seed or wool. Upon returning to Mora, the craftsmen, in turn, sold the goods for cash.

Frequently other salesmen would come to Mora and buy large quantities of carved horses to use as gifts, barter items, or payment for room and board as they traveled throughout the country selling their wares. Although it is not known exactly how much they had to pay for the

Horse from Morgedal, Telemark.

Toy horse.

©yfjell Bygdemuseum, Telemark.

Horse carved by Anne Hellem, ca. 1825.

Gransherad Bygdemuseum, Telemark.

horses, it was, at any rate, cheaper for them to pay for their lodgings with wooden horses than to use cash, and apparently the horses were readily accepted as payment wherever they traveled.

Demand for the horses became so great, therefore, that large-scale production became common, even in the 1840s. As noted earlier, the carving was done by craftsmen, and specialists did the painting. Anders Nisser, the son of the well-known early twentieth-century painter Mor Nisser, estimated that he had to shoot as many as fifteen to twenty squirrels per year just to keep his mother supplied with enough squirrel hair to make the brushes she used to paint the horses.

The production of Dalecarlian horses has continued right up to the present. Since 1928, nearly all of the figures have been made in and around the village of Nusnäs, near Mora. Although modern technology is now used both in sawing out the figures and in some aspects of the painting process, each figure is still carved by hand by local craftsmen and receives its painted decoration by hand as well. Not only are the horses sold in Sweden and throughout the rest of Europe, but they are also sent to shops in Japan, Australia, Canada, and the United States.

It is clear that there has been a folk-art tradition of carving small human and animal figures for at least the past two to three hundred years, especially in Sweden. Three-dimensional figures were sometimes created as part of a decorative whole (lions on doorposts, for example). Other figures were carved as freestanding utilitarian objects (toys, human figures used as candle holders, bird-shaped drinking vessels, and so on). Still other figures were created as pieces of representational, nonfunctional art, but they were probably made by carvers who found figure carving to be nothing more than an enjoyable pastime. And then along came Axel Petersson Döderhultarn. ...

The world-famous Dalecarlian Horse.

Nordiska Museet, Stockholm

Candle holders from Östergötland, Sweden.

Candle holder from Ringebu, Gudbrandsdalen, Norway, now at Maihaugen, Lillehammer.

CHAPTER 2

Scandinavian Figure Carvers

Among a long list of Scandinavian figure carvers, several stand out. We now turn our attention to these outstanding carvers.

Axel Petersson Döderhultarn

Axel Petersson has been called a natural genius. He was born in the parish of Döderhult near Oskarshamn in 1868. His figures, which typically depict the peasants and village folk around whom he grew up and lived, have earned him the reputation as one of Sweden's greatest artists.

Even as a boy, Petersson exhibited considerable artistic talent both at home and in school. His talent was never encouraged, however, and his only training stemmed from a brief informal apprenticeship under a local woodcarver and sculptor, Edward Källström. His primary interest lay in whittling or sculpting small figurines, an activity considered a worthless pastime by his neighbors as well as his family.

His family finally decided that young Axel should emigrate to America, where he would be forced to stand on his own two feet and make something of himself. So, money was provided and off he went. But he didn't get farther than nearby Malmö, where instead of purchasing a ticket to America, he spent most of his travel money on lottery tickets and partying.

Opposite: by Axel Petersson Döderhultarn.

Upon his return to Oskarshamn, where his widowed mother had moved in 1889, he continued his figure carving. Much to the dismay of his family and acquaintances, carving remained his primary activity. For nearly twenty years, he lived in relative isolation, venturing out only occasionally to attend social gatherings or to sell his inexpensive wooden figures at the local market in Oskarshamn.

As he had been taught by Källström, Petersson carved in a rather naturalistic style during the beginning of this period. His early work, often in pear wood and rendered in quite a traditional style, was typically sanded. Although the style of his work defies a systematic chronology, sometime around 1900 he developed more of a rough-hewn, flat-plane, or minimalist style. Using a knife and just a few gouges, he began carving figures in alder. Upon completion, many of his figures were then painted in subdued colors.

Petersson's six- to fifteen-inch-tall figures portray local peasants engaged in everyday activities: milking a cow; attending a funeral, wedding, or baptism; having their picture taken by a photographer; and so forth. It's been said that he also derived inspiration from medieval wooden sculptures in churches, caricatures drawn by the famous Swedish artist Albert Engstrom, and illustrations in various publications, including some that were Norwegian.

Axel Petersson Döderhultarn.

In 1909 Petersson was invited to participate in a caricature exhibition in Stockholm. Public response to his work was immediate and overwhelming. In the newspaper *Dagens Nyheter (News of the Day)* on January 20, 1909, art critic Georg Nordensvan wrote: "Axel Petersson's old men are irresistibly amusing. They depict such primitive art as one could wish for, made out of a couple of simple contours using only a couple of strokes, but, from an artist with sure eye and nimble hands. It is a new conception with a personal touch … small masterpieces of complete nonconformative art." As can be said of a great cartoonist or caricaturist, he had mastered the difficult art of simplification—saying more by saying less.

Following closely on the heels of the exhibition in Stockholm, some of Petersson's figures were purchased by Swedish art museums, lending even further legitimacy to the artistic merit of his work. He also began receiving requests to have his work exhibited throughout the rest of Europe and in the United States. Hailed as "Döderhultarn" (the man from Döderhult), he started using that name in addition to Axel Petersson.

In 1910 his work was shown in Paris. In 1911 it was exhibited in Brighton, Copenhagen, Rome, Turin, Stockholm, and Malmö. Fifty-seven figures were also shown in Oskarshamn, and a museum association was formed there to lay the groundwork for a Döderhultarn Museum. In 1912 some of his work was shipped to the United States, where the Swedish Consulate sent it on

Boys playing with carved wooden figures, including two of Döderhultarn's, circa 1913.

Army Horse, by Döderhultarn.

Finger Hooking, by Axel Petersson Döderhultarn.

Dancers, by Axel Petersson Döderhultarn.

Döderhultarn in his studio.

Peasant, by Axel
Petersson Döderhultarn.

a tour of several cities, including New York, Buffalo, Toledo, Chicago, Boston, and San Francisco.

Döderhultarn's prominence as a "high artist" is well documented and accepted. However, at the same time that his work was being exhibited internationally and purchased by museums, he continued to carve figures for local sales.

The photo of the two boys outdoors with the carved wooden figures (on page 30) is from the archives of the Döderhultarn Museum and is believed to have been taken in 1913. The photo suggests that the boys were using the wooden figures as toys. The two human wooden figures clearly appear to be the work of Döderhultarn. The photo had been mailed, without an accompanying note, to Döderhultarn, possibly as a way of thanking him or as proof that the figures that had been ordered had arrived and were indeed being used.

Beginning in 1908, Döderhultarn's figures were sold through the Handcraft Association in nearby Kalmar. The store continued to serve as his local sales outlet, even after the artist had achieved international fame.

A postcard sent to Döderhultarn by the store in 1915 features a photo of the store's interior, showing several

of the artist's carvings on the counter. On the back of the postcard, the store placed yet another order with the carver. Individual figures sold for approximately ten kronor (U.S. $1.50–$2.00), while groupings sold for thirty to forty kronor.

Photos of Döderhultarn's figures were widely circulated. Articles about, and reviews of, his exhibitions often included drawings of his work, and postcards featuring his carvings were available at least as early as 1912, if not earlier.

It has been said that Döderhultarn was unique. It seems that his uniqueness lay not in that he was one of the first to carve figures in this style, but rather in that he was the first essentially self-taught figure carver to be accepted or discovered by the art world. Döderhultarn stood firmly planted in the world of folk art, carving wooden figures destined for use as children's toys— but he also carved similar figures for exhibition in art museums and galleries throughout Europe and America.

Photo Bukowskis auctions.

Auction, by Axel Petersson Döderhultarn.

Auction detail.

Photo Bukowskis auctions.

Grazing Cow, by Axel Petersson Döderhultarn.

Photo Bukowskis auctions.

Old Man, by Axel Petersson Döderhultarn.

Photo Bukowskis auctions.

Maid with a Cow, by Axel Petersson Döderhultarn.

Photo Bukowskis auctions.

Galloping horses, by Axel Petersson Döderhultarn.

Old Man and Woman, by Axel
Petersson Döderhultarn.

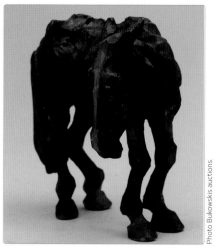

Dark horse, by Axel Petersson Döderhultarn.

Standing Accordianist, by Axel
Petersson Döderhultarn.

Seated Accordianist and Dancing Couple, by Axel Petersson Döderhultarn.

Herdsman and Cow, by Axel Petersson Döderhultarn.

Herdsman with Cattle, by Axel Petersson Döderhultarn.

Standing Cow, by Axel Petersson Döderhultarn.

Man with Cane, by Axel
Petersson Döderhultarn.

Auction detail.

Old Woman, by Axel Petersson Döderhultarn.

Man with Calf, by Axel Petersson Döderhultarn.

Photo Bukowskis auctions

Auction detail.

Photo Bukowskis auctions

Seated Accordianist, by Axel Petersson Döderhultarn.

Photo Bukowskis auctions

The Christening, by Axel Petersson Döderhultarn.

Döderhultarn's Influence on Other Carvers

Döderhultarn's influence on other carvers should not be underestimated. Because photos and drawings of his work were so readily available and widely circulated, they undoubtedly served as inspiration for countless other carvers in Scandinavia and abroad.

A "Döderhultarn figure" became a generic term for any small wooden figure rendered in a minimalistic style. For example, a souvenir stand near Oskarshamn hung out a sign some years ago advertising Döderhultarn figures. When asked if the figures for sale were actually carved by Axel Petersson, the proprietor replied that, of course, they weren't carved by Axel Petersson, but because of the style and subject matter, they were indeed Döderhultarn figures.

The simplicity of Döderhultarn's figures comprised an art form with which common folk could easily identify. The people, who had grown up in a tradition in which practically every male was at least somewhat skilled with a knife, apparently felt that they too could create "Döderhultarn figures," even though they may not have had any art training. For instance, in a letter to Döderhultarn in 1922, a resident of a home for the elderly in Sundbyberg, Sweden, wrote that he was

looking for a hobby to help pass the time. Because he had done some woodworking years ago, he said, he was interested in working in wood, perhaps in making some small figures. Then he went on to ask for Döderhultarn's assistance and advice.

The popularity of Döderhultarn's figure carving among common folk quickly spread beyond his own country. Evidence of this can be seen from an article in the September 28, 1913, issue of the widely read Norwegian magazine, *For Bygd Og By (For Country and Town),* which described the work of a figure carver named Ragnvald Einbu from Gudbrandsdalen. The writer, apparently without any need for further explanation to the general readership of the magazine, compared the Norwegian artist to "the well-known Axel Petersson, Döderhultarn, from Småland in Sweden."

Another Norwegian, Sverre Johnsen (1844–1939) created, among other pieces, Döderhultarn-style figures. According to the Lexicon of Norwegian Artists, Johnsen was called "Norway's Döderhultarn." Johnsen was, however, only one of many who carved small individual figures or groupings depicting such themes as a drinking

Wedding, by Axel Petersson Döderhultarn.

Detail from The Christening.

party, card players, or a chorus and was compared to Petersson.

In the United States and Canada, where hundreds of thousands of Norwegians and Swedes had emigrated only a few decades earlier, figure carving had also become popular. The late Dr. Marion Nelson, professor of art history at the University of Minnesota and former director of Vesterheim, the Norwegian-American Museum in Decorah, Iowa, wrote in 1989: "In doing research … it became evident that there was a lot of small figure carving among the Norwegians in our area about 50 years ago. The subjects were immigrant[s] and pioneer[s] …"

Despite the lack of written documentation indicating that Döderhultarn's carvings directly influenced other carvers, several of his subjects and designs can clearly be recognized in the work of later carvers. One is obviously Oscar Sjögren, an artist who emigrated from Emmaboda, Sweden, in the 1920s and settled near Duluth, Minnesota. Not only did he create figures in a style reminiscent of Döderhultarn's, but he also featured some of the same subjects, such as a wedding scene and a photographer.

Photos and sketches of pieces by H. S. "Andy" Anderson, the well-known American caricature carver, suggest that he too had seen pictures of Döderhultarn's work (page 58). Anderson, in turn, went on to influence other American figure carvers, including Harold Enlow (page 59). Enlow states that when he began carving, his initial inspiration came from Anderson's book, *How to Carve Characters in Wood*.

Although many carvers drew much of their inspiration from Döderhultarn's work, this should not minimize in any way their own creativity and artistic talent. Everyone derives inspiration from one source or another. As I mentioned earlier, Döderhultarn's work has served as an inspiration for my own work as well. It is merely interesting to note that his influence has been enormous and far-reaching right up to the present.

Petersson was once asked how he felt about other carvers emulating his work. Did he mind? Did he regard them as unwelcome competition? No, he said, he wasn't threatened in the least. "There are thousands of snuffbox carvers out there, but there is only one Döderhultarn!"

Carl Johan Trygg

It has been said that it's often only fate that determines which artist becomes the standard-bearer of a new style of art. Axel Petersson became known as the father of Döderhultarn figures, but perhaps they could have been called "Trygg figures" instead.

Born in 1887 in Skagerhult, near Örebro, C.J. Trygg began carving wooden figures as a boy. As one of nine children in a poor family, he had to quit school and leave home at the age of twelve to earn money to supplement the family's income. But he continued to carve rough-hewn figures that depict the types of folk he knew from his background—primarily Swedish farmers, laborers, preachers, policemen, and seamen.

Even though C.J. Trygg began carving figures before Döderhultarn's 1909 Stockholm exhibition, the figures of Trygg, who was nineteen years younger than Döderhultarn, were similar in style to Döderhultarn's and extremely well done.

At first Trygg was unable to make a living from just the sales of his carvings and had to carve on a part-time basis while working at other jobs. But eventually, perhaps in part because of an exhibition of his work in Stockholm in 1915, he was able to devote himself full-time to his carving.

Trygg enjoyed telling a story about the initial purchase of his work by an art dealer in Stockholm. The dealer's wife had wanted her husband to purchase a dozen figures, but the dealer only purchased three. The next day, Trygg, who had never met the art dealer in person, dressed up in his finest and went to the shop, where he promptly bought all three of his own figures. The day after that, the dealer contacted Trygg and ordered two dozen figures. Through the years, this dealer continued to be Trygg's best customer in all of Stockholm.

Together with his three sons, Carl Olof, Nils, and Lars, who were also figure carvers, Trygg immigrated to Canada in the 1930s. There, C.J. and sons, especially Carl Olof (born in 1910), apparently met with considerable success. While their figures had been earning them only a few crowns each in Sweden, they were fetching up to $20 apiece in Canada.

Both C.J. and C.O. Trygg eventually returned to Sweden, however, where they continued their careers. C.J. is said to have carved well over ten thousand figures before his death in 1954. Much of the Tryggs' work can be found in private collections in Canada and the United States as well as in Sweden.

Hobo, by C.J. Trygg.

Sailor, by Lars Trygg.

Logger, dated 1930, by C.O. Trygg.

Many Trygg figures have the family name carved on the front of the base.

Lars Trygg apparently had a commercial outlet for his carvings, some of which are stamped with "A Peer Import Sweden."

Carl Johan Trygg signed many of his figures with his initials and the family name.

Carl Olof Trygg usually signed his carvings with the country where a figure was carved as well as the date.

Many Trygg carvings are signed "Handcarved by Trygg." These may be the work of Carl Johan Trygg.

Curler, A Peer Import Sweden, by Lars Trygg.

Hobo, Sweden 1975, by C.O. Trygg.

Man in Topcoat, 1939, by C.J. Trygg.

Man in Vest, Sweden 1920, by C.J. Trygg.

Captain, Sweden 1980, by C.O. Trygg.

Man in Top Hat, by C.J. Trygg.

Man in Vest, by C.O. Trygg.

Photo by Roger Schroeder.

Woman with Cup, by Trygg family.

Photo by Roger Schroeder.

Farmer, by Lars Trygg.

Photo by Roger Schroeder.

Three Happy Friends, by Nils Trygg.

The American-Swedish Institute, Minneapolis, Minnesota.

Man in Boat, by C.O. Trygg.

Woman in Shawl, Sweden 1980, by C.O. Trygg.

Monk, Sweden 1960, by C.O. Trygg.

Cowboy, by Trygg family.

Golfer, Canada 1920s, by C.J. Trygg.

Splitting Wood, by C.O. Trygg.

Photo by Roger Schroeder

The American-Swedish Institute. Minneapolis. Minnesota

Oscar Sjogren

The Photographer,
by Oscar Sjogren.

The Male Chorus, by Oscar Sjogren.

Paul Bunyan, by Oscar Sjogren.

At the Fishmarket,
by Oscar Sjogren.

Peasantry Wedding, by Oscar Sjogren.

Born Josef Oscar Sjögren and raised near Emmaboda, Sweden, Sjogren (1883–1964) immigrated to Superior, Wisconsin, in 1922. He was employed as a commercial artist in nearby Duluth, Minnesota, but woodcarving was his lifelong passion. Drawing on memories of friends and neighbors back in Sweden as well as folks from the Duluth-Superior area for his models, Sjogren was yet another carver who created figures in a minimalist style.

Although his figures are somewhat more refined than those of Döderhultarn, they clearly show knife and gouge marks and portray some of the same rural characters and situations featured in Döderhultarn's pieces. His work is represented in numerous private and museum collections. The largest collection of Sjogren figures and groupings is owned by the St. Louis County Historical Society in Duluth, Minnesota.

Man in Coat, by Oscar Sjogren.

Man with Pipe, by Oscar Sjogren.

Two Figures, by Oscar Sjogren.

Herman Rosell

Herman Rosell (1893–1969) was another self-taught Swedish carver who created small figures and groupings that depict rural life in the nineteenth century. His abilities as a carver and caricaturist were highly regarded, and in addition to participating in exhibitions both in Sweden and abroad, his work was featured in a film on Swedish television in 1959.

Although his subject matter is similar to Döderhultarn's, his style of carving is more refined. Rosell stated that he became familiar with Döderhultarn's work only after he had carved for many years and developed his own style.

In addition to pieces in Sweden, a number of Rosell's figures can be seen at the American-Swedish Institute in Minneapolis, Minnesota.

The American-Swedish Institute, Minneapolis, Minnesota.

Fiddler and Woman, by Herman Rosell.

The American-Swedish Institute, Minneapolis, Minnesota

Immigrant Couple, by Herman Rosell.

Rosell images courtesy The American-Swedish Institute, Minneapolis, Minnesota

Three Women Having Coffee, by Herman Rosell.

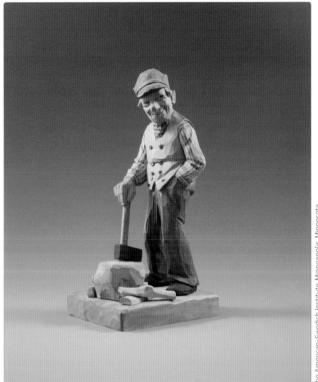

Man with Pipe, by Herman Rosell.

Chopping Wood, by Herman Rosell.

Couple at Museum, by Herman Rosell.

Emil Janel

Born Emil Nygård in 1896 near Orsa, Sweden, this gifted artist began to attract attention even as a very young boy when he started whittling small wooden animals. Despite a lack of any formal training, he continued to carve and paint, and at nineteen years of age was awarded first prize at a national sculpture exhibition in Stockholm.

Recognizing his artistic abilities, both Carl Milles, a well-known Swedish sculptor, and Anders Zorn, a painter, invited Emil to study with them. But the young artist's parents would not allow it, stating that he had to help his father with his job as a woodcutter and part-time ranger.

In 1923 Emil traveled to Winnipeg, Canada, where he joined his brother and began working as a lumberman. Eventually he moved to Seattle and then to San Francisco, where he lived for the rest of his life. It was when he moved from Canada to the United States that he adopted the surname "Janel," after the famous turn-of-the-century sports figure, John L. Sullivan. He had been told that his Swedish name, Nygård, was too difficult and confusing for non-Scandinavians to pronounce.

Working primarily in unseasoned alder, Janel carved his fifteen- to twenty-four-inch figures using only a mallet, gouges, and a knife, holding the figures between his knees. As with Döderhultarn's and other Scandinavian figure carvers' work, with which he undoubtedly was familiar, Janel's characters, typically tall and thin, depict common folk going about their everyday activities. Frequent subjects were laborers, immigrants, and loggers he had encountered. However, he did not carve in an angular, flat-planed, minimalist style, but rather his work has been categorized as "exaggerated realism."

During the first years he lived in the United States, he had to earn part of his livelihood from jobs other than his carving. But eventually he supported himself through his carving alone, especially after he began his association with Maxwell Galleries of San Francisco. In 1965 Janel was awarded the Royal Order of Vasa by His Majesty King Gustav Adolph VI of Sweden in recognition of his work as an artist. He died in San Francisco in 1981.

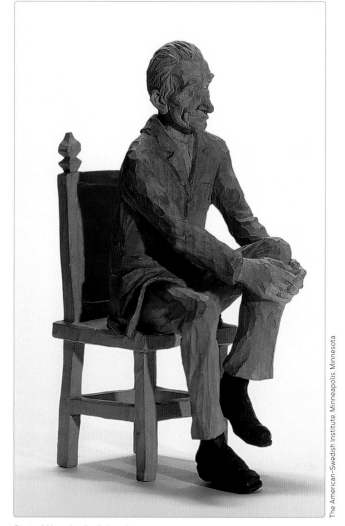

Seated Man, by Emil Janel.

Man with Walking Stick, by Emil Janel.

Monk, by Emil Janel

Two Men, by Emil Janel.

Thelma "Telle" Rudser

Despite the fact that it was primarily men, rather than women, who attained notoriety as figure carvers, there were certainly a few female carvers. It is true, however, that in an earlier era, handwork activities were quite gender specific. The Norwegian researcher and writer Halfdan Arneberg authored a richly illustrated two-volume work on handcraft in Norway in 1951. Volume I, titled *Men's Work*, dealt with work in wood and metal; the second volume, *Women's Work*, focused on textiles.

But there were exceptions, and Telle was one of them. Born in 1910 into a Norwegian-American family in Grand Forks, North Dakota, she began to carve and sell wooden figures to earn money while she was a student at the University of North Dakota. After graduation, she continued her craft-related work as a recreation leader for the Grand Forks park system and for the WPA. In 1943

she enlisted in the U.S. Navy. While she was a trainee at Hunter College in New York, an exhibition of her carvings was arranged, but during the night before the exhibition opened, all of her carvings were stolen.

After the war ended, Telle moved into a small house in tiny McKenzie, North Dakota. She erected a large sign on the roof that read "Telle's Hobby Lab," where she continued to carve animals—especially dogs—and Norwegian-inspired caricatures, until her death in 1981.

Sven and Urban Gunnarsson

When Sweden's late Prime Minister Olof Palme visited Cuba, he took a gift for Fidel Castro: a wooden caricature of the bearded Cuban leader, carved by Sven Gunnarsson.

Gunnarsson (1909–1985) began carving figures as a boy. His rough-hewn, flat-plane figures depicted rural folk and clearly recognizable political leaders.

"Gunnarsson figures" were also carved by Sven's brothers Nils and Olof, and by a son, Peder (1936–1968).

In the 1960s Gunnarsson was joined by his son Urban, who was then fifteen. At their shop on Drottninggatan in Stockholm, Gunnarsson figures used to be painted by Urban's mother, Ursula, and later by his sister, Gisela.

Seaman, by Gunnarsson.

Churchill, by Gunnarsson.

Man with Cap, by Gunnarsson.

Martin Engseth

Born in Norddal, Møre-Romsdal, Martin Engseth (1903–1972) emigrated from Norway to America in 1926. In addition to working as a rosemaler (rose painter), Engseth also carved figures, much in the spirit of other figure carvers of the time in Norway, Sweden, and Scandinavian America.

Photo Darrell Henning

Photo Darrell Henning

The Wood Gatherer, by Martin Engseth.

The Woodchopper, by Martin Engseth.

Bjarne Walle

From the outset of his adult life, Bjarne Walle (1911–1989) wanted to make woodcarving, especially figure carving, his career. Although his flat-plane figures sold for more than 30,000 kroner ($4,000–$5,000) at his first major exhibition in 1945, the artist from Bamble, Norway, also had to work as a carpenter. His desire to tell stories, however, both through his carved figures and his writing, was so strong that he often carved or wrote during his lunch breaks. It was not until 1970 that his income from figure carving and writing allowed him to devote himself to them full-time.

Walle's painted figures, typically larger and less angular than those of Döderhultarn, often feature trolls or people in humorous situations. His carvings, as with the many stories and books that he wrote, usually have "happy endings." It's been said that Walle couldn't bring himself to allow bad things to permanently befall his characters.

Saturday Night by Bjarne Walle.

Henning Engelsen

A carver of trolls, Norwegian rural folk, Vikings, fishermen, animals, and characters from Nordic mythology, Henning Engelsen (1918–2005) lived and worked at Kapp, in Toten, about 75 miles (120 km) north of Oslo. Engelsen began creating his flat-plane style "Henning figures" in 1947, and he led the company until 1988. The workshop is now run by some of his descendants. Henning figures continue to be popular souvenir items throughout Norway as well as abroad, especially in the United States.

Miner, by Henning.

Bridal Pair, 1956, made for Husflid by Henning, Norway.

Bridal Pair, 1956, made for Husflid by Henning, Norway.

Milking Time, by Henning.

Fisherman, by Henning.

Anton Pearson

The Swedish-American carver Anton Pearson, born in 1892, began carving as a young boy in his hometown of Lund, Sweden. His interests eventually led him to study at the Technical School in Lund, after which he immigrated to America in 1912. It is said that he tried to book passage on the *USS Titanic*, but all of the tickets for that particular crossing—when the ship sank—were already sold. Following years of adventurous travels throughout the eastern United States, he eventually settled in Lindsborg, Kansas—home to many fellow Swedish immigrants—where he studied art at Bethany College, met and married Grace Lane, and established the woodcarving studio in which he worked until his death in 1967. His figures, carved with knives he made himself, often depicted fellow hard-working immigrants. In 1952 the Pearsons' daughter, Rosemary, married woodcarver/artist Norman Malm (1928–2011), who eventually succeeded his father-in-law. The Malms' son Jim has continued the family's carving tradition.

Woman carved by Anton Pearson, Lindsborg, Kansas.

Man, by Anton Pearson.

Man carved by Anton Pearson, Lindsborg, Kansas.

Other Scandinavian Carvers

The list of carvers whose work has just been reviewed does not even presume to be complete but merely provides a sampler. If we were compiling a complete list, figure carvers such as Gudleik Brekhus, Styrk Fjose, Ragnvald Einbu, Axel J. Persson, Sverre Johnsen, Lorens Larsson, Hans Sorken, "Ole the Hermit," John Altenborg, "Grandma Larkin," Iver Anderson, and countless others would have been included as well.

By the early 1980s, most of the figure carvers who had been working in Döderhultarn's style back in the 1920s and 1930s—probably the height of its popularity—were no longer alive. Only a few bearers of the flat-plane, Döderhultarn-influenced tradition remained.

Photo Courtesy of Rauland Dansarring

Figure carver Aslak K. Svalastoga, Rauland, Telemark.

Sveinung Svalastoga: porch pillar at Svalastoga home, Rauland, Telemark.

Photo Norma Refsal

Carving by Olav Bakken, Gransherad, Telemark.

Lårdal Bygdemuseum, Telemark

Lady with Goat, by Olav Tveito, Vinje, Telemark.

The Tippler by Sverre Johnsen, 1870-1900.

The Tippler, detail.

Norwegian Packhorse, by Sjur Mørkve, Voss, Norway.

Immigrant, date unknown, by Ole Olson.

Carving by Kolbein Hommedal, Indre Arna, Norway.

Man with Walking Stick, 1970, attributed to Andre Barr Gould.

Modern Tradition: Richard Rolander

Richard Rolander, born in Rockford, Illinois, in 1927, began working in wood at an early age. His appreciation for the handwork of Sweden eventually lead him to import Swedish antiques and collect old and new Dala horses. He also used his wood-related skills to create pieces of his own inspired by Swedish traditional art, including Dala horses. His carved horses were typically painted by two different painters, one in Illinois, another in Sweden.

His work attracted attention when he sold some of his painted horses at a market in Sweden. In 2001, Grannas Olsson Hemslöjd—a Swedish company well known for Dala horse production—commissioned Rolander to carve a limited-edition horse in their "new copies of antique horses" collector's series. That first horse, aptly named *Rolander*, sold out. There followed a series of limited-edition horses, with a different horse every year or so. Altogether, more than 500 of these horses have been sold in Sweden.

Sadly, in 2013 Rolander lost nearly all of his eyesight, and so was forced to quit carving horses. But, as with other carvers, his work continues to please and inspire.

Rolander, 11", was the first limited-edition collector's horse sold at Grannas Olsson, Nusnäs, Sweden. Carved by Dick Rolander and painted by Marianne Bågling, Sweden; 2002-2003.

Havet, 8½", is the last horse carved by Dick Rolander before he lost his eyesight. Painted by Diane V. Johnson; dated 06/2013.

Piggy Bank, 5½", was carved and painted to resemble a photo of an old Swedish bank. Painted by Marianne Bågling, Sweden; 2006.

Andy Anderson

Herbert S. "Andy" Anderson, born in 1893 in Chicago, Illinois, became a sort of Pied Piper. His homespun western magnetism attracting a parade of carvers who continue to leave a trail of wood chips not only nationally, but internationally, into the 21st century. Andy didn't leave much of a written record as to the source of his inspiration. However, figure carvers can read in his work the suggestion that he drew at least some of his inspiration from the carving of Axel Petersson Döderhultarn, whose work was exhibited in several cities around the United States—including Chicago—when Andy was young. A museum professional in Sweden, familiar with Döderhultarn's work, remarked when he saw photos of some of Andy's carvings for the first time, "It looks like that horse of Andy's is a descendant of one of Döderhultarn's horses."

Andy's flat plane, minimalist style was ideal for carving some of the rough-around-the-edges cowboys he encountered after moving to Colorado, and later, California. His fascination with the Old West inspired countless carvings, many of which wound up in various art collections. Some were purchased and given as gifts to dignitaries around the country, including President Franklin D. Roosevelt. He died in Sante Fe, New Mexico, in 1960.

Many fine carvings by Andy Anderson can be seen at the Stark Museum of Art in Orange, Texas.

Carved wooden bust of Andy Anderson

Doctor and Patients

Doctor, Nurse and Patient

Shotgun Wedding

Cow, Boy and Horse

Harold Enlow

Harold Enlow began whittling as a child in the Ozark Mountains. Stationed in Okinawa as a young GI, he carved anything he could get his hands on, including wood from pallets and crates. And then a friend lent him a book by Andy Anderson entitled *How to Carve Characters in Wood*. Harold was fascinated. As his carving skills grew, he began to convert some of Andy's caricatures into not only cowboys, but also mountain folks modeled after the people he remembered from back home.

Figure carving eventually became Harold's profession. In addition to selling his carvings, roughouts, and teaching aids, he wrote numerous instructional books and taught as many as 40 classes per year throughout the United States and Canada. Harold was a founding member of the Caricature Carvers of America in 1990 and named the first *Woodcarving Illustrated* Wood Carver of the Year in 2000.

Harold, therefore, has inspired countless other carvers, many of whom have gone on to teach seminars and workshops themselves.

The trail of woodcarving chips continues…

Harold Enlow

Mama Don't Allow No Guitar Playing Around Here!

Uncle Bigun

Harold Enlow began carving mountain folk when he was living far from his home in the Ozarks.

Sneakin' Past the Sheriff portrays the mountain folk of Harold's youth.

Like Andy Anderson, Harold Enlow has long carved cowboys and their broken-down horses.

Harley Refsal

I have included, here at the end of this chapter, a sampling of my own pieces carved in the flat-plane style. Many of my carvings are based on my knowledge of Scandinavia, both from a historical standpoint and from personal experience, as I have traveled there often.

Half-hour Before Sunup, by Harley Refsal.

The New Schoolmaster, 1988, by Harley Refsal.

Scandinavian Kick Sled, by Harley Refsal.

The Ice Fisherman, 1990, by Harley Refsal.

Another Season, 1984, by Harley Refsal.

Heading Home, 1988, by Harley Refsal.

Farmer, 1987, by Harley Refsal.

Nisse Mor and Nisse Far, 1991, by Harley Refsal.

Skiing, 1990, by Harley Refsal.

Taming the Prairie, 1987, by Harley Refsal.

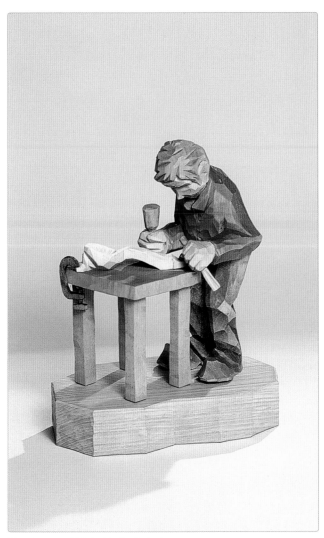

Woodcarver, 1990, by Harley Refsal.

The Tomte, 1991, by Harley Refsal, painted by Karen Jensen.

The Knife Makers, 1989, by Harley Refsal.

Photo: Arne Aas

Mocha Mary, 2014, by Harley Refsal.

Photo Scott Kriner

Java John, 2013, by Harley Refsal.

Photo Scott Kriner

Class of '38, 2013, by Harley Refsal.

Photo courtesy Emily Voss

Newlyweds, 2013, by Harley Refsal.

Karl Oskar, 2003, by Harley Refsal. Featured in the video *Figure Carving Scandinavian Style with Harley Refsal.* (See bibliography page 77.)

Troll Queen, 2011, by Harley Refsal.

Troll King, 2004, by Harley Refsal.

Father Christmas, 2003, by Harley Refsal.

Swenson Family Fiddlers, 2012, by Harley Refsal.

CHAPTER 3

Carving a Traditional Dalecarlian Horse

As you've undoubtedly noticed while reading through the first two chapters, flat-plane carvings are just that: carvings that derive their shapes from a series of flat planes.

In this chapter you will be able to follow step-by-step photos, accompanied by explanatory text, as I carve a stylized horse using only a single knife. Although this critter is my own design, he/she is obviously inspired by the traditional wooden horse carved for nearly two centuries in the Swedish province of Dalarna (also known by the Latinized version of that name, Dalecarlia). See pages 22 to 27 for more information about and photos of Dalecarlian Horses.

It should be noted that the carving of wooden horses was common and popular throughout Scandinavia—not just in Sweden—but it is the Dalecarlian Horse that has become the most widely known throughout the world.

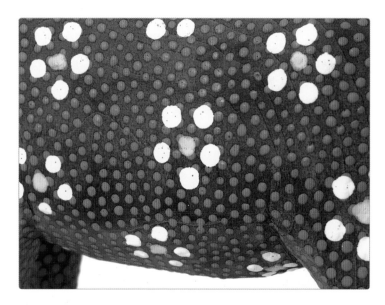

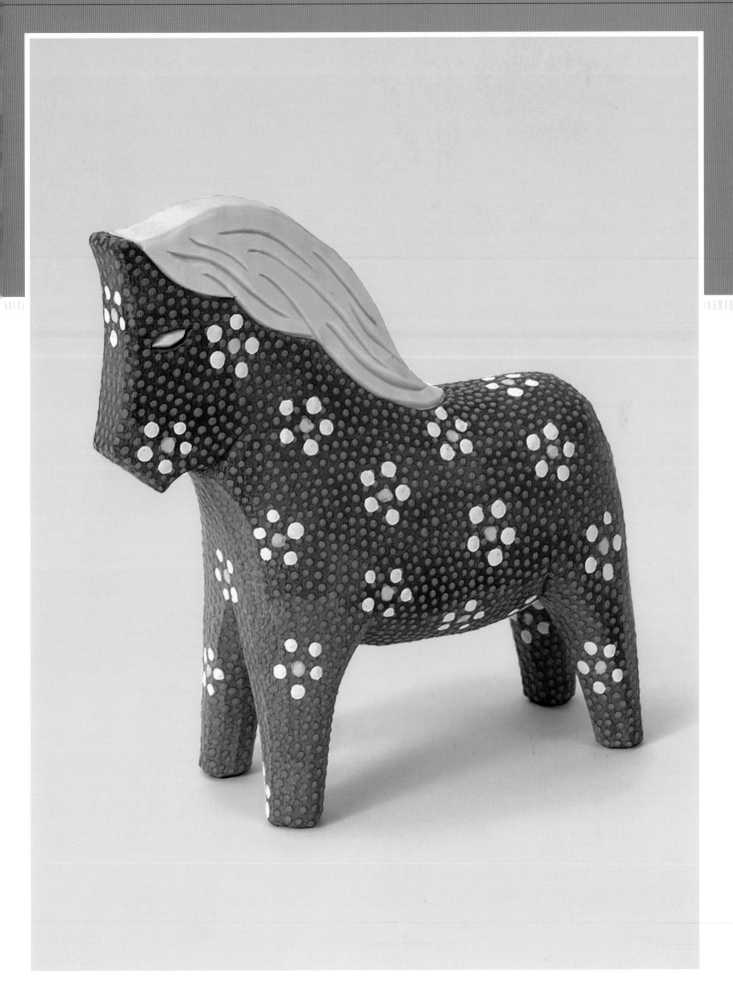

Basic Carving Instructions

For two centuries, the government of Norway, trying to protect its artisan guilds, forbade the common people from owning and using any tools other than an axe and a knife. Although we assume some people used illegal tools, the majority simply became very skilled with the two available to them.

Flat-plane carving developed from that tradition, so most flat-plane projects, including the four horse patterns in this book, can be carved with just a sharp knife. However, I cut the pattern outlines with a saw to save some hand carving, and I occasionally use a gouge or V-tool for details.

About Knives

Some carvers use a folding pocket knife, but I prefer a fixed-blade knife, which typically has a more comfortable handle. More important than the style of knife is keeping it sharp; a sharp knife is actually much safer to work with than a dull one. Keep your knife sharp by using a strop. I strop at least once an hour using aluminum-oxide powder on leather. Also, I highly recommend wearing a Kevlar carving glove while you work.

Choosing Materials

I use basswood for my carvings because it is easy to carve and paint, and will hold detail. If you want to use a different wood, I suggest pine. Poplar is a little too stringy and, because of its dominant grain, butternut does not work well for painted pieces. I carve most figures with the wood grain running up and down; that alignment will add strength to the horses' legs.

Transferring the Pattern

To start any carving, size the pattern as desired and measure it to determine the proper size for the wood blank. Use carbon or graphite paper to transfer the pattern to the wood. You can also make a fresh photocopy of the pattern, place it facedown on the wood, and apply either dry heat (such as an iron or woodburning tool) or acetone to the back to transfer the lines to the blank.

Getting Started

Cut around the outline using a band saw, scroll saw, or coping saw. If necessary, refer to the pattern to refresh any pattern lines that were cut off, or to add details.

Carve the general shape of the entire figure before adding any details. If you develop one section prematurely and carve all of its details before blocking in the rest of the figure, you may find you have one or more elements in the wrong place in relation to the rest of the carving. Then, you have to carve that section away and start over, or live with a poorly carved figure.

Finally, remember to take your time. Hasty work can result in a mistake on your carving or an accident with one of your tools.

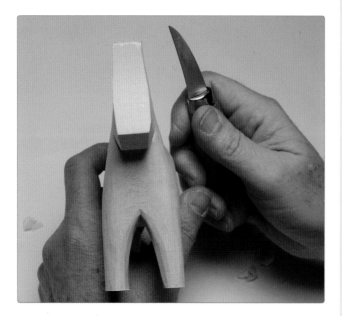

CARVING TIPS

- Rough out the anatomy first to maintain the carving's balance and proportion. Carve the details later.

- Refer to the pattern regularly because you may need to redraw reference lines several times. Keep the big picture in mind. Details are meant to be done last.

- As an advanced carver, I remove large chips. If you are a beginning carver, it is fine to make small cuts at first. Control is more important than removing large chunks of wood.

- It is okay to fix your mistakes. Some accidents can lead you in a direction that is much more interesting than your original idea.

- Remember to stop and strop frequently. You should strop at least once an hour. I use aluminum-oxide powder on leather.

- Carve in good light. If carving outdoors, in natural light, the best light seems to be what I call open shade. Avoid direct sunlight and intense shade.

Painting and Finishing

As much as I enjoy carving a piece, I also enjoy painting it. It's always surprising how long a good paint job takes. Don't rush the process—depending on the complexity of the piece, the painting time can almost rival the time needed to carve.

I use basswood for most of my projects. Light in color and lacking a strong figured grain, basswood is easy to carve and ideal for painting. I prefer to use acrylics diluted with water to create a wash, because I want the wood grain to show through the paint.

I paint with a chisel, or angle, brush because it allows me to reach the corners and edges of the carving. A liner brush is helpful to paint very small areas, get into the tiniest of corners, and for fine detail work.

Mixing a Wash

To mix paint washes, pour a small amount of water—only a few teaspoonfuls—into a container, and then add a few drops of paint. Most of the paint containers I use have a top that can dispense individual drops. You can use an eyedropper if desired. Stir the paint and water together, and then test the mixture by painting on newspaper. The newsprint should be easily visible through the color wash. If the mixture is too thin, continue to add paint, drop by drop, and keep testing until you achieve the desired result.

Painting a Carving

Check that you have a clean cut between areas of different colors. I keep a knife handy to correct cuts between the colors if needed.

Start painting on the back of the carving or in some other less noticeable area. Beginning to paint in an inconspicuous place enables you to get used to the feel of the brush and paint on wood. This approach helps you become more comfortable with painting before moving on to a more difficult or more noticeable area.

Create a strategy before you begin. Acrylics dry quickly, so start with a color that can dry while you paint the next part. Avoid painting next to a still-wet color. If you would rather not wait for paint to air dry, use a hair dryer to speed up the process.

Finishing a Carving

I finish my horses with a thin coat of Delta Ceramcoat clear all-purpose sealer. You can also spray them with clear polyurethane. For other figures, I use Johnson Paste Wax, following the instructions on the can. Brush it on, and then wipe off the excess wax with paper towels. Use a toothpick to remove any embedded wax bits to avoid them hardening in deep, hard-to-clean areas. Then, buff or wipe the carving with a soft cloth.

PAINTING TIPS

- When you are done carving, check that you have carved away all of the raw wood. Uncarved wood accepts paint and finish differently than carved wood and will be visible on the finished project.

- If you notice pencil or oil marks on the completed carving, wash it with soap and water, rinse it thoroughly, and let it dry before you paint it.

- Paint light colors before painting adjacent dark colors. Dark paint will layer over light paint, but not vice-versa. Let each color dry before painting the adjacent areas.

- I make color washes by mixing 5 to 7 drops of water per 1 drop of paint. For lighter washes, use 10 drops of water to 1 drop of paint. Use full-strength black and white paint for the eyes.

- Dalecarlian Horses are generally painted in bright colors with flower motifs. You are welcome to use your favorite colors and combinations, of course.

Carving the Horse

MATERIALS

- Basswood, 2" (51mm) thick and sized to match pattern
- Acrylic paint: blue, orange, yellow, white, or colors of your choice
- Paint sealer, such as Delta Ceramcoat clear all-purpose

TOOLS

- Carving knife
- Band saw, scroll saw, or coping saw
- Paintbrush
- Paperclip

1 Cut the blank. Transfer the pattern (page 74) to the wood and cut it out using a band saw, scroll saw, or coping saw. Using a pencil, extend the lines of the front and back legs.

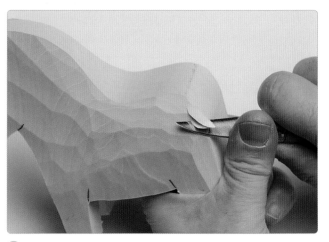

2 Round the corners. Begin removing wood from the back of the horse. Simply round off all of the corners to start.

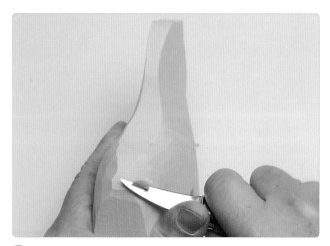

3 Carve the sides. Continue removing wood on the sides of the horse to produce a rounded effect.

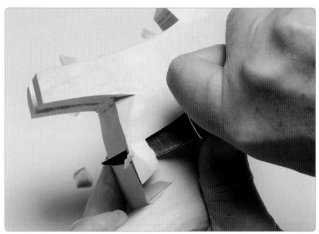

4 Carve the belly. Remove wood from the underside of the horse. Remove wood in long cuts to round off the edges.

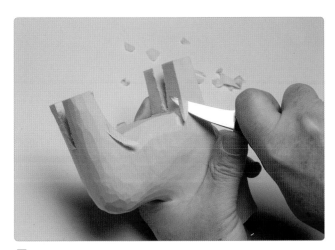

5 Shape the legs. Round the legs by removing the corners. Remember, make a minimum of long cuts.

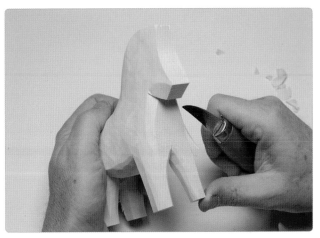

6 Carve the chest. When the legs are rounded, move to rounding off the chest.

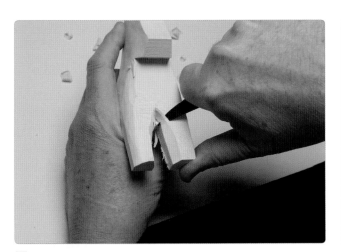

7 Detail the legs. Clean up the joint between the front legs and the joint between the back legs.

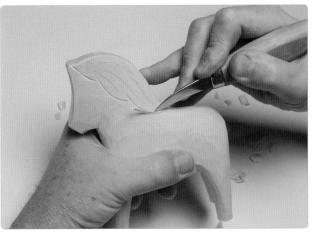

8 Carve the mane and tail. Use the tip of the knife to cut in details for the mane and tail. Check that all of the wood has been carved, and clean up any rough cuts.

Painting the Horse

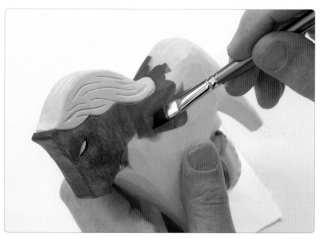

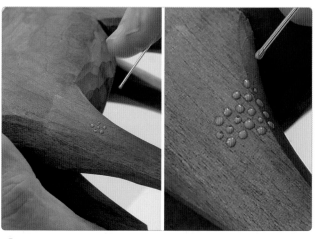

1 Mix and test the body paint. Mix 1 drop of blue acrylic paint with 5 drops of water. This is a bright, but thin mix. Begin painting in an inconspicuous area to ensure that the mix is correct. I chose the underside of the horse.

2 Paint the base coat. Paint the horse. I start at the face and work my way back to the hind end, painting the legs and belly last. The mane, tail, and eyes remain unpainted. Acrylic paint dries very fast, so paint the entire base coat in one sitting. Stopping in the middle then restarting may leave an unsightly line where the dry and wet paints meet.

3 Practice the polka dots. I decorated this horse with contrasting polka dots. To make the dots, straighten a paper clip, dip the end into a puddle of undiluted orange acrylic paint, and then touch the paper clip to the surface of the horse. Practice on paper until you are comfortable with the technique.

4 Paint the polka dots. Begin by making a row of two or three dots about ⅛" (3mm) apart. Expand the dot pattern to a rosette, and then continue adding dots in a systematic manner. Make the dots as evenly spaced and as evenly shaped as possible. Of course, they won't be perfect, but they should be close.

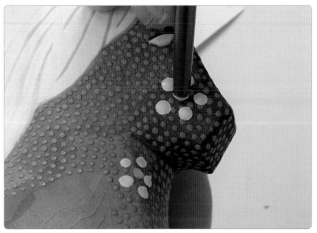

5 **Add the flowers.** Use larger dots to create a stylized floral pattern over the dots. Start by dipping the end of a paintbrush into undiluted white paint and touching it to the surface of the horse. Paint the eyes with undiluted white, as well.

6 **Dot centers in the flowers.** Use undiluted yellow paint in the same manner to create the center of the flower. Continue making polka dots and flowers until the carving is completely covered.

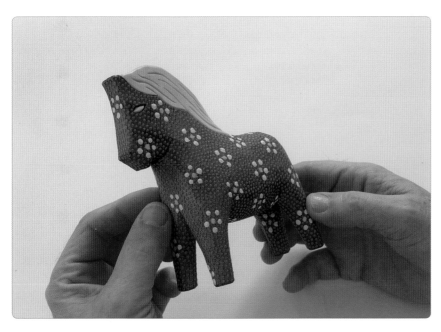

7 **Seal the carving.** Let the carving dry thoroughly. Brush on a thin coat of Delta Ceramcoat clear all-purpose sealer. The sealer is optional, but it will help the wood of the unpainted mane and tail keep its natural color.

Patterns

Horse 1

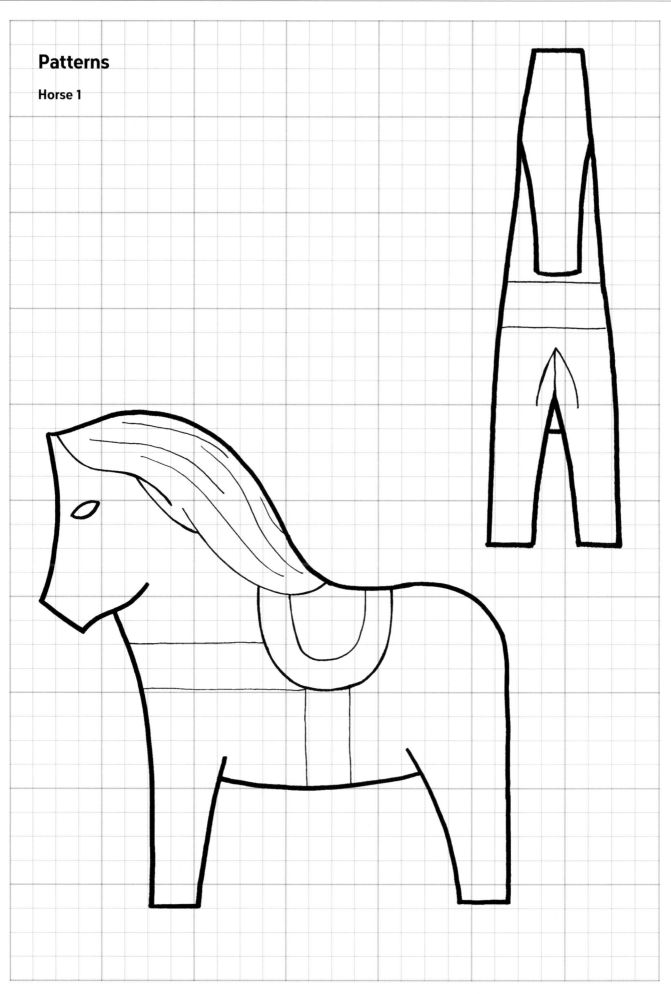

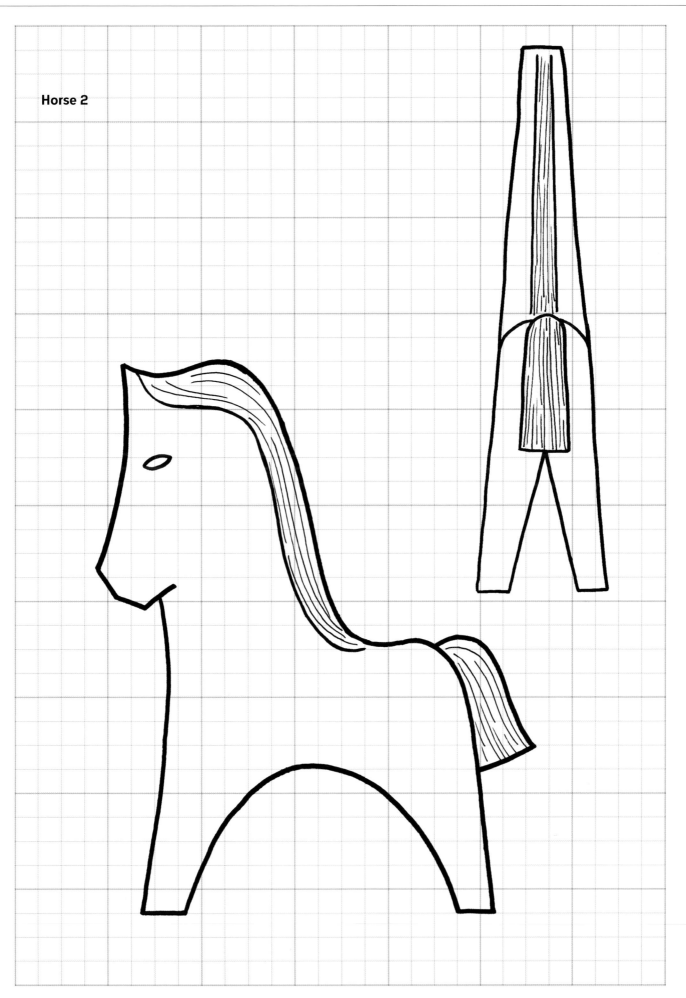

Horse 2

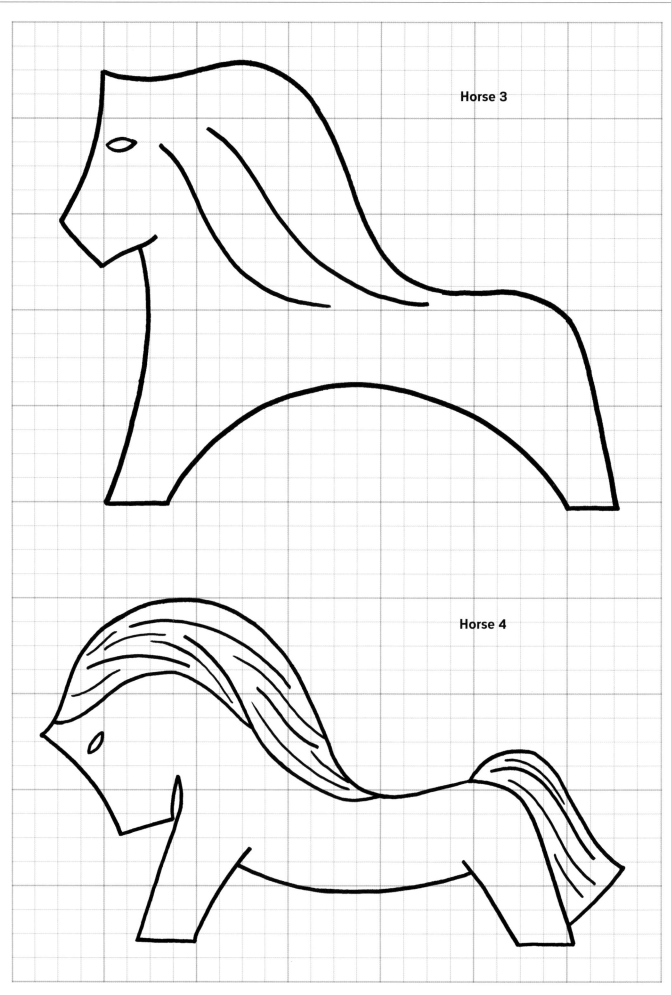

Horse 3

Horse 4

Bibliography

Döderhultarn, Axel Petersson, and Det Är Något Särskilt med Trä, articles in *Hemslöjden* 1991/ 2 (pp. 9–11) (written in Swedish). Stockholm: Olle Nessle and Mark Esping, 1992.

Figure Carving Scandinavian Style with Harley Refsal. 2004. Produced by Pinewood Forge, Leonard, MN. Videocassette/DVD.

Henning, Darrell, Marion Nelson, and Roger Welsch. *Norwegian-American Wood Carving of the Upper Midwest* (written in English). Decorah, IA: Vesterheim, 1978.

Magerøy, Ellen Marie. *Norsk Treskurd* (written in Norwegian, contains English summary). Oslo: Det Norske Samlaget, 1983.

Mosey, Chris and Michel Hjorth. *Magic Horse.* Stockholm: BOOX, 1999.

Nylén, Anna-Maja. *Swedish Handcraft* (English translation of Hemslöjd, written in Swedish). Lund: Håkan Ohlssons Förlag, 1976.

Rådström, Anne Marie. *Dalahästen* (written in Swedish). Hedemora: Gidlunds Bokförlag, 1991.

Refsal, Harley. *Carving Trolls and Other Scandinavian-Style Characters.* Decorah, IA: Dog Hill Press, 1995.

Refsal, Harley. *Whittling Little Folk: 20 Delightful Characters to Carve and Paint.* East Petersburg, PA: Fox Chapel Publishing, 2011.

Weissman, Ira, and John Matthews. *Master American Woodcarver Emil Janel* (written in English). New York: New York Woodcarving Press, 1984.

Swedish rooster, carver and date unknown.

Courtesy the Nordic Heritage Museum, Seattle, WA

Bieschke collection. Photo by Erin Kirkpatrick. Rockford. Ill.

Evening Star, or Aftonstjäma in Swedish, was carved by Dick Rolander and painted by Diane V. Johnson. The horse is 13" tall and dated 2003.

Acknowledgments

The Swedish Institute (Stockholm), Döderhultarn Museum (Oskarshamn), Norwegian Foreign Ministry (Oslo and New York), Norwegian Folk Museum (Oslo), Viking Ship Museum (Oslo), Nordmanns-Forbundet (Oslo), Norway-America Association (Oslo), Maihaugen (Lillehammer), Akademiet (Rauland), E.L.C.A.-Faculty Research Grant (Chicago), Sons of Norway (Minneapolis), American-Swedish Institute (Minneapolis), Vesterheim (Decorah), Bukowskis, and Luther College (Decorah) have all provided me with financial and/or moral support in connection with my research. To them as well as to my family, friends, and countless other museum staffers, librarians, and woodcarvers, I extend my sincere appreciation.

Except in the step-by-step demonstrations and as noted otherwise, all of the photographs were taken by Chip Peterson, Julie Strom Hendrickson, or my wife, Norma Refsal (who also painted many of my carvings).

Index

Note: Page numbers in *italics* indicate illustrations/photographs.